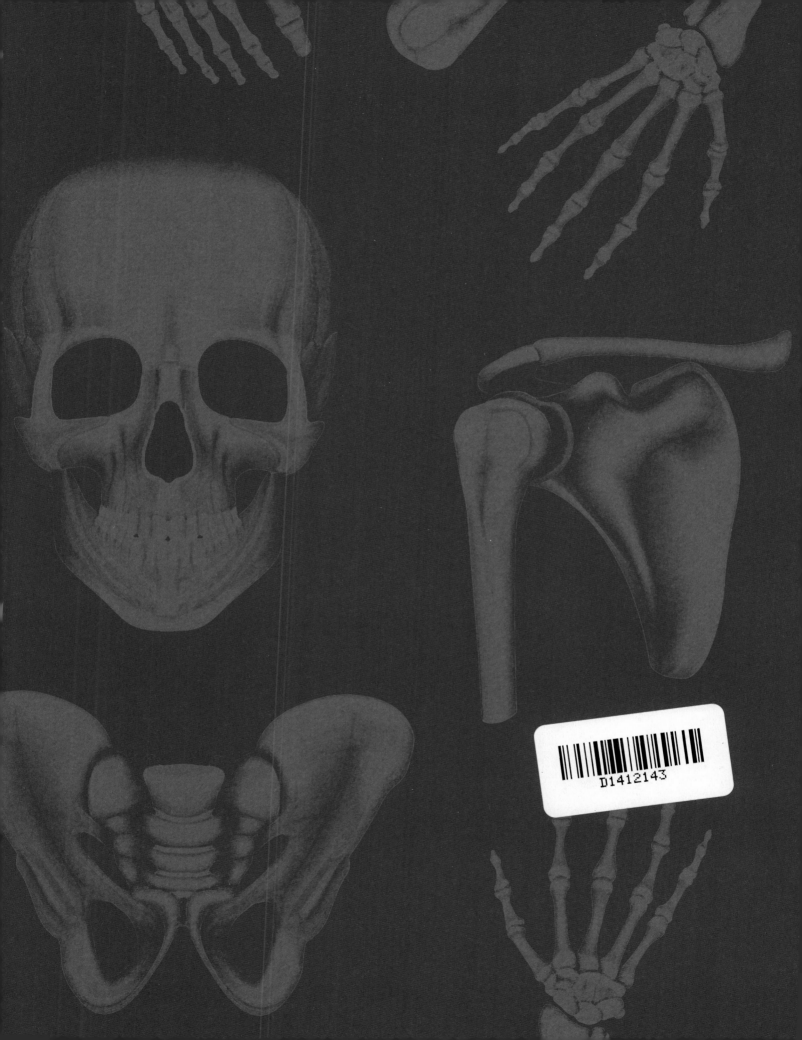

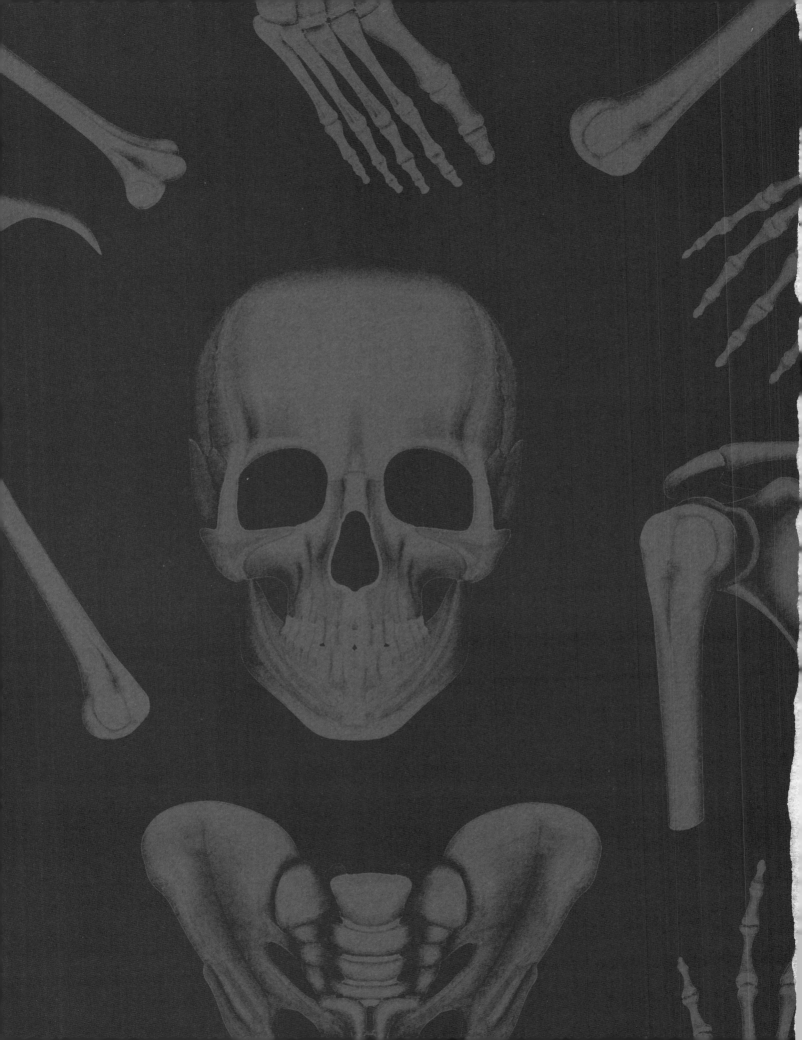

{ Femur }

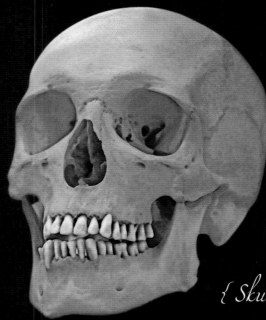

{ Skull }

Bone Collection
HUMAN BODY

{ Hand }

{ Torso }

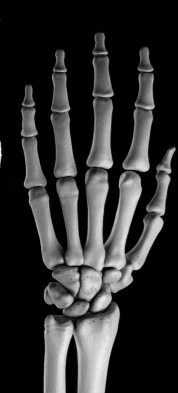

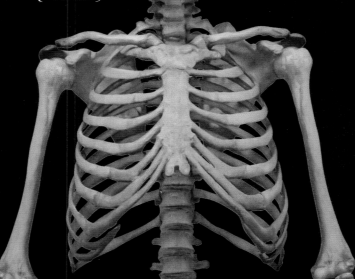

{ Spine }

Silver Dolphin Books

An imprint of Printers Row Publishing Group

10350 Barnes Canyon Road, Suite 100, San Diego, CA 92121

www.silverdolphinbooks.com

Written by Rob Colson

Illustrated by Elizabeth Gray, Steve Kirk, Simon Roulstone and Dynamo

Paper Engineering and Model Illustration by Geoff Rayner/Bag of Badgers Ltd.

Printers Row Publishing Group is a division of Readerlink Distribution Services, LLC.

Silver Dolphin Books is a registered trademark of Readerlink Distribution Services, LLC.

All notations of errors or omissions should be addressed to Silver Dolphin Books, Editorial Department, at the above address. All other correspondence (author inquiries, permissions) concerning the content of this book should be addressed to Quarto Children's Books Ltd, The Old Brewery, 6 Blundell Street, London N7 9BH UK.

ISBN: 978-1-68412-327-8

Manufactured, printed, and assembled in Shaoguan, China.

First printing, December 2017. SL/12/17

21 20 19 18 17 1 2 3 4 5

PICTURE CREDITS

Bone Collection
HUMAN BODY

Silver Dolphin

CONTENTS

{ Shoulder and arms }

INTRODUCTION

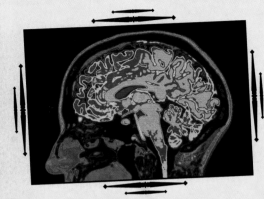

{ Brain }

THE human body is a marvel of coordination and teamwork, as trillions of tiny **cells** work together in **systems** to keep humans alive. The body is built around a bony skeleton, which gives strength and shape, protects

{ Facial hair }

organs, and allows the body to move. The digestive system breaks down food so the body can absorb it. Food is then turned into energy, which allows the body to move, think, grow, and stay healthy. The heart beats without a break, pumping blood to every part of the body. The blood carries food and oxygen to cells and attacks any germs in its way. Senses provide information about the world, which the brain then processes. The whole system is under the control of the brain, a complex structure that gathers information and constantly makes decisions about what to do next. From head to toe, get ready to explore the human body!

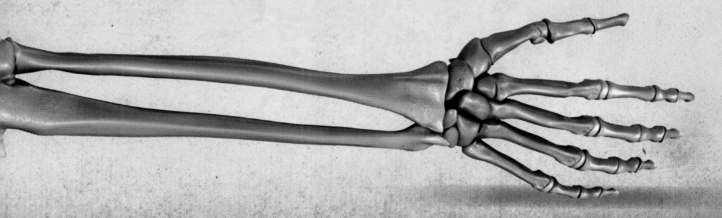

BODY STRUCTURE

EVERY second of every day, the human body performs an amazing range of jobs. It takes in energy and uses it to grow and repair itself, and generally stay alive. These jobs are performed by a wide range of structures from cells to systems such as the digestive and respiratory systems.

CELLS

The smallest structures in the body are cells. They come in a wide range of shapes and sizes depending on their function.

The human egg, or ovum, is the largest human cell.

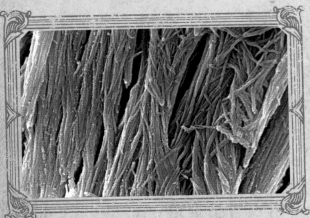

{ Bone tissue }

TISSUE

Cells of the same type join together to form **tissues**. Each tissue performs a specific role. For example, muscle tissue contracts or shortens to pull on body parts.

ORGANS

Different tissues combine to form organs. The kidneys are organs that filter and clean the blood to remove unwanted substances.

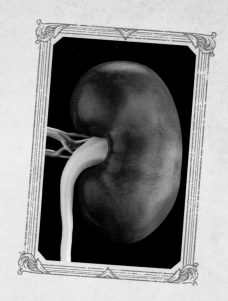

{ Kidney }

SYSTEMS

These are collections of organs and other parts that perform complex jobs. The circulatory system transports blood around the body.

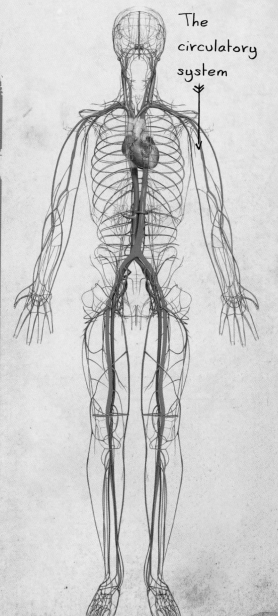

The circulatory system

STUDYING BODIES

Hundreds of years ago, the only way to study the insides of a human body was to cut one open. Today, high-tech scanners are used to create pictures of the inside of the body without having to use knives.

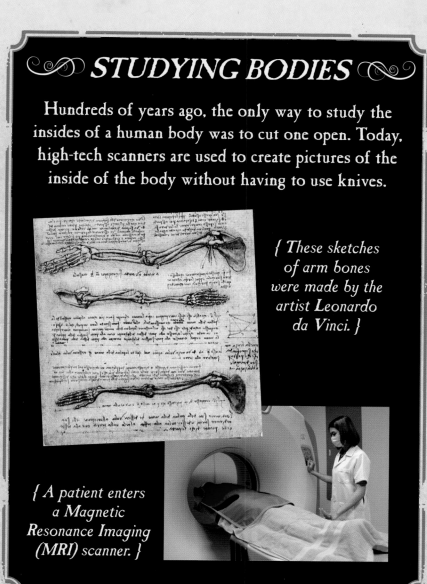

{ These sketches of arm bones were made by the artist Leonardo da Vinci. }

{ A patient enters a Magnetic Resonance Imaging (MRI) scanner. }

BUILDING BLOCKS

THE human body is made from trillions of tiny cells. Each cell performs a particular job. The body constantly makes new cells to replace old ones.

Nucleus is the cell's control center

Identical Twins

Identical twins develop from a single fertilized egg cell, which then divides into two. The cells in their bodies contain the same sets of genes, which means that they develop to look and behave just like one another.

TISSUES AND ORGANS

Similar kinds of cell organize themselves into groups called tissues. Tissues form larger body parts called organs.

Cell **membrane** protects the cell and controls which substances can enter it.

Mitochondrion releases energy to power the cell.

CODE FOR LIFE

Inside the nucleus of every cell are 46 long molecules called **chromosomes**. These each contain about 25,000 instructions that tell the cell what to do. The instructions are called genes and they provide a complete code for creating life.

Chromosomes are made from a substance called DNA. The DNA forms twisting strands in a "double-helix" structure.

Cytoplasm is a jelly-like fluid that fills the cell.

SKELETON

HUMANS walk on two legs. This frees up the hands to explore the world. In order to make full use of the hands, a big brain helps humans to think and solve problems.

ALL-AROUND ATHLETES

Humans can run, jump, swim, climb, and throw. These skills allow humans to survive in many different kinds of habitats.

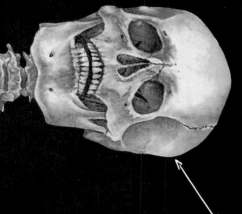

The rounded skull protects the large brain. The skull is made of 22 bones. Of these, 21 are fused tightly together to make a hard case. Only the hinged jawbone can move.

RIB CAGE

The rib cage is a framework of bones that protects the lungs and heart. With each inhale, muscles pull at the rib cage to make it larger, pushing air into them.

Elbow

Bowl-shaped hip bones

The thigh bones are angled to place the legs right under the body. This makes walking on two legs much easier.

Baby Bones

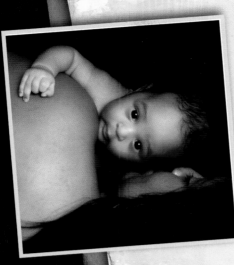

A newborn baby's skeleton is made of more than 300 bones. As the baby grows, some of these bones join together. An adult human skeleton has just 206 bones.

BUILD YOUR OWN
HUMAN BODY
SKELETON
AT THE END OF THE BOOK!

↙ There are 26 bones in each foot.

Long thigh bone

Kneecap

FLEXIBLE THUMBS

The thumbs have flexible **joints** that allow them to touch any of the fingers. This allows humans to pick up objects and turn them around in their hands to examine them.

There are 27 bones in each hand.

Flat feet with short toes provide a solid platform for walking.

WHAT'S IN BONES?

Bones are made of different kinds of tissue, which make them strong enough to support the body, but light enough to move. Weight for weight, bones are five times stronger than steel.

THE STRUCTURE OF A BONE

The outer layer of a bone is made of hard **compact bone**. Under this is lighter, **spongy bone**. The center of the bone is hollow and contains blood vessels and yellow **marrow**.

FAT STORES
Yellow bone marrow is a store of fat.

Blood vessels

{ Spongy bone }

Compact bone

LIGHT AND STRONG
The honeycomb structure of spongy bone makes it light but strong.

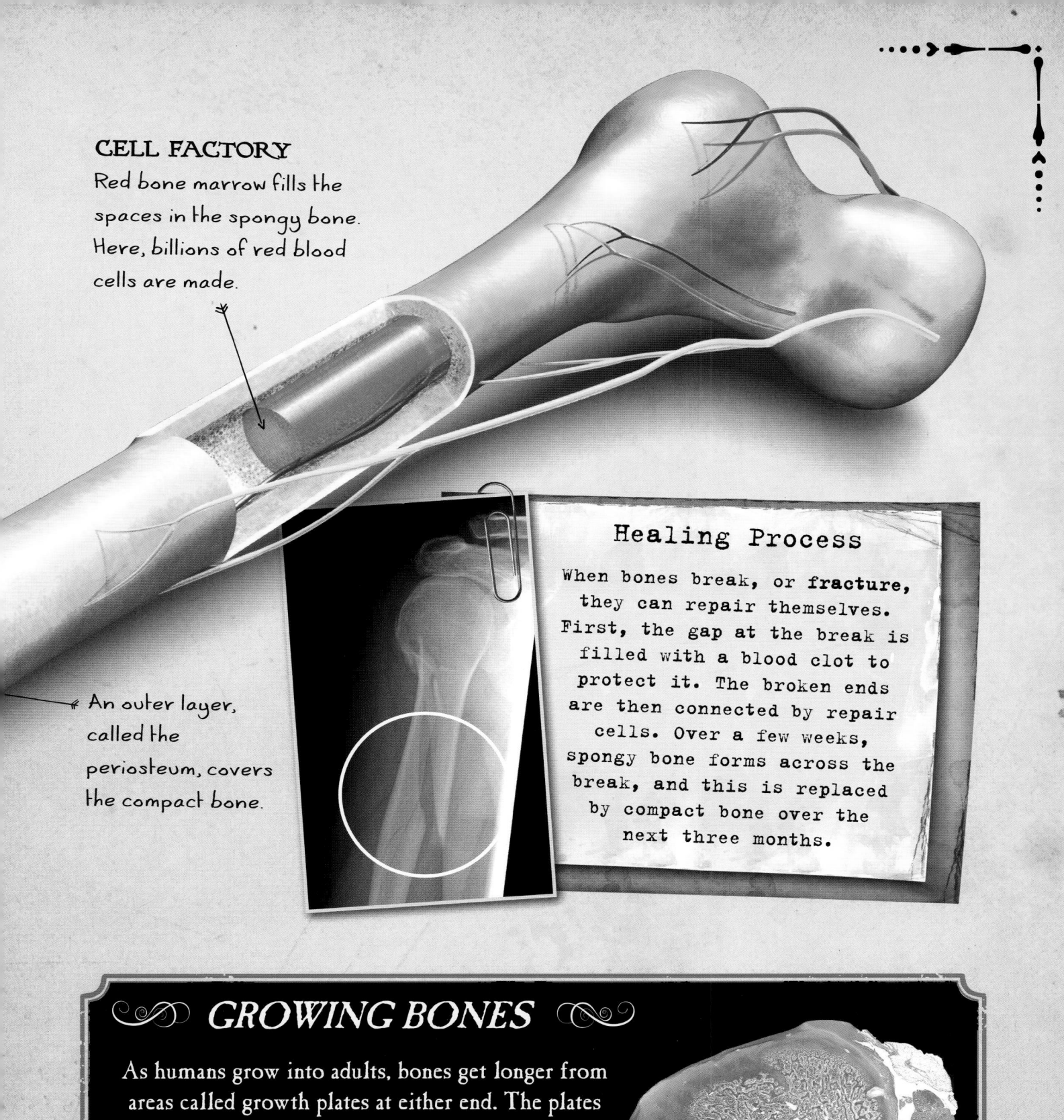

CELL FACTORY

Red bone marrow fills the spaces in the spongy bone. Here, billions of red blood cells are made.

An outer layer, called the periosteum, covers the compact bone.

Healing Process

When bones break, or **fracture**, they can repair themselves. First, the gap at the break is filled with a blood clot to protect it. The broken ends are then connected by repair cells. Over a few weeks, spongy bone forms across the break, and this is replaced by compact bone over the next three months.

GROWING BONES

As humans grow into adults, bones get longer from areas called growth plates at either end. The plates produce soft cartilage, to which minerals such as calcium are added so that they harden into bone.

{ The cartilage growth plates enable the bone to grow longer. }

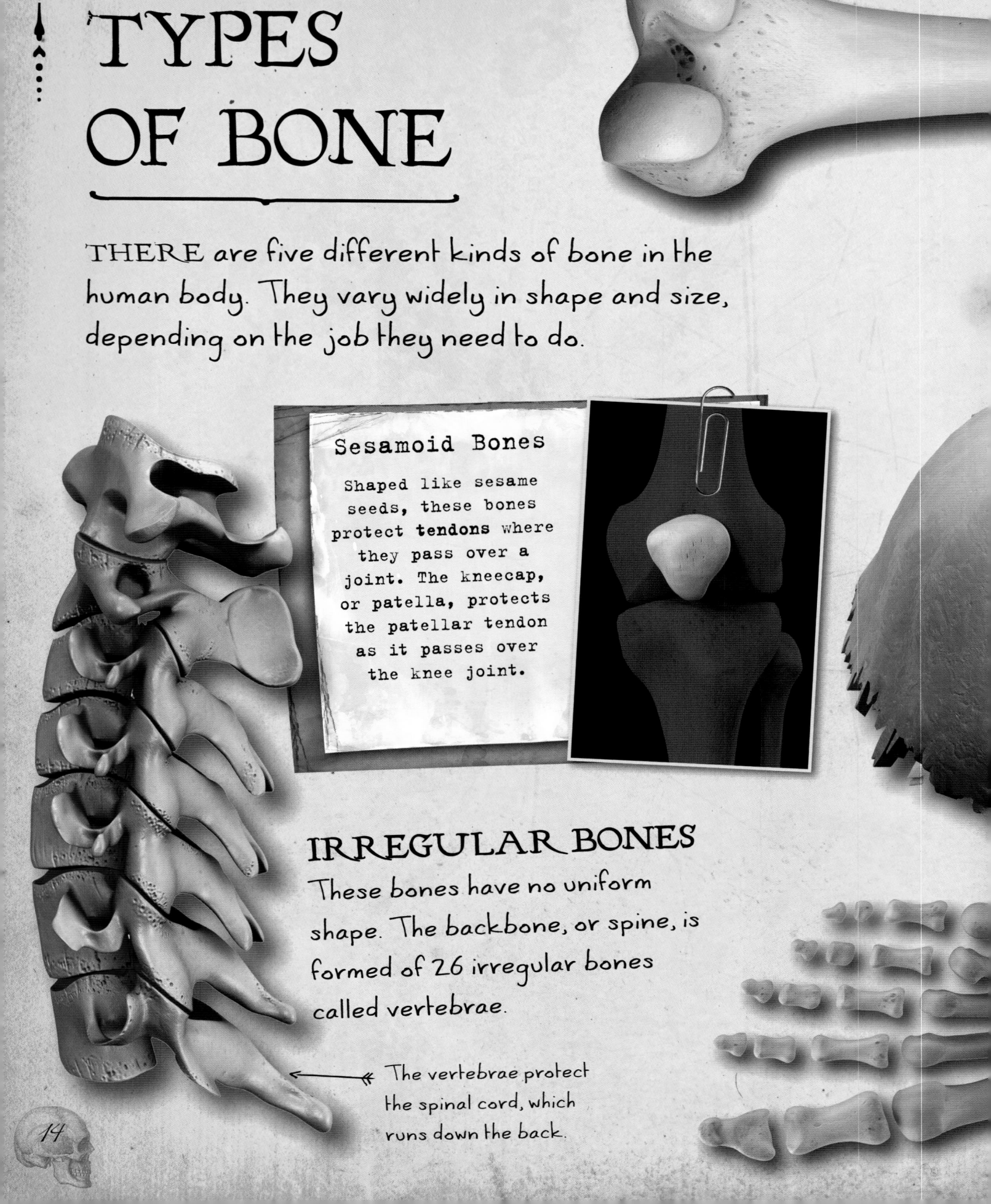

TYPES OF BONE

THERE are five different kinds of bone in the human body. They vary widely in shape and size, depending on the job they need to do.

Sesamoid Bones

Shaped like sesame seeds, these bones protect **tendons** where they pass over a joint. The kneecap, or patella, protects the patellar tendon as it passes over the knee joint.

IRREGULAR BONES

These bones have no uniform shape. The backbone, or spine, is formed of 26 irregular bones called vertebrae.

The vertebrae protect the spinal cord, which runs down the back.

LONG BONES

Long bones support the body and allow movement. They include the largest bone in the body, the femur, or thigh bone, and the small phalanges, the finger and toe bones.

Frontal bone

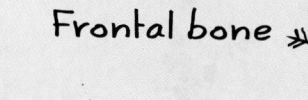

FLAT BONES

Flat bones are thin and usually curved. They protect vital organs, such as the brain.

Parietal bone

Cuboid bone

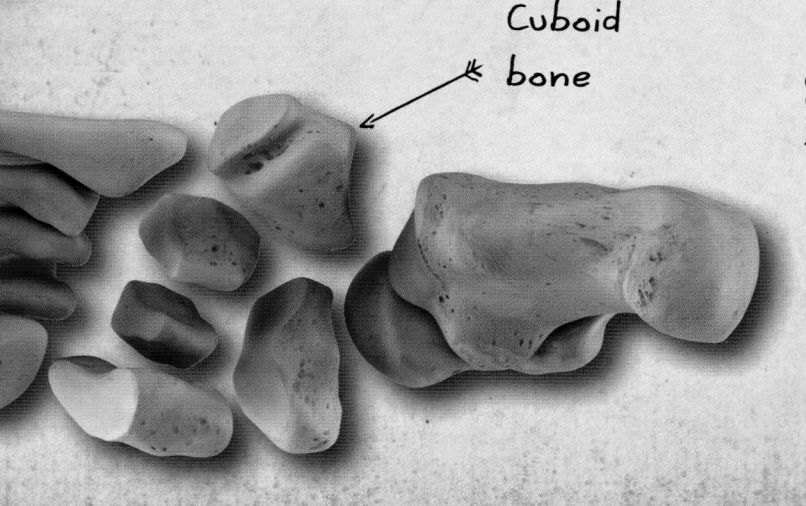

SHORT BONES

The cube-shaped short bones are found in the wrists and ankles. They provide support and stability, but very little movement.

JOINTS

THE places where bones meet one another are called **joints**. There are more than 400 joints in the human skeleton. Most joints allow for movement, but some fix the bones firmly in place.

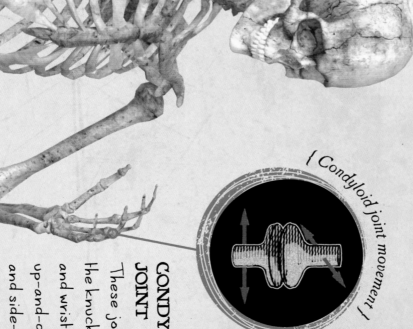

{ Saddle joint movement }

SADDLE JOINT

The thumb is attached to the hand with a saddle joint. This allows thumbs to move with a hinge-like motion and also to rock from side to side.

{ Pivot joint movement }

MOVABLE JOINTS

There are six kinds of movable joints.

PIVOT JOINT

Pivot joints allow the bones to rotate. Pivot joints in the neck allow the head to turn from side to side.

{ Condyloid joint movement }

CONDYLOID JOINT

These joints in the knuckles and wrists allow up-and-down and side-to-side movements.

SEMIMOVABLE JOINTS

The joints in the hipbones allow only limited movement. They are held together by cartilage.

{ Ball-and-socket joint movement }

BALL-AND-SOCKET JOINT

Found in the hips and in the shoulders, ball-and-socket joints allow movement in most directions.

{ Hinge joint movement }

HINGE JOINT

The elbows and knees have hinge joints. These work like the hinges on a door, allowing for a swinging motion to bend or straighten arms or legs.

PLANE JOINT

Found in the joints between the small bones in the ankle and wrist, plane joints allow small but flexible movements as the bones slide against one another.

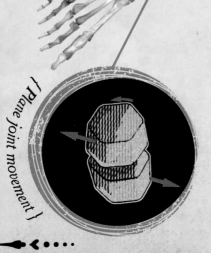

{ Plane joint movement }

FIXED JOINTS

Skull bones are fused tightly together by fixed joints called sutures. Teeth are held in their sockets by special cement and tough fibers called ligaments.

{ Skull bones }

{ Teeth }

SKIN, NAILS, AND HAIR

THE skin provides a protective outer layer to bodies. It is waterproof, germ-proof, and can repair itself. Hair and nails, made of dead cells, grow out of the skin.

LARGEST ORGAN

The skin is the largest organ in the human body. An average adult human's skin weighs around 10 pounds. If laid out flat, the skin would cover an area of 22 square feet.

Protective Nails

Nails protect the tips of our fingers and toes, and help us to grip small objects. They grow slowly at about 0.1 inches per month.

ON THE SURFACE

The outer layer of the skin, the **epidermis**, is made largely of flat cells packed with tough keratin. Dead skin cells are constantly being shed from the epidermis and replaced by new ones.

Blood vessels

HAIR

The human body is covered with millions of hairs, which grow out of follicles in the skin's **dermis**. Hairs grow at different rates depending on where they are. A man's beard grows fastest of all, adding about 0.015 inches of length per day.

Epidermis

BENEATH THE SURFACE

The thicker dermis contains blood vessels, sweat glands, and hair follicles. Nerves in the dermis sense temperature, touch, and pain, and send messages to the brain.

Hair follicle

Nerve ending

Layer of fat

FINGERPRINTS

Tiny ridges at the ends of the fingers help to grip objects. The pattern these ridges make is called a fingerprint. Each person's fingerprint has a unique pattern.

SKULL

HUMANS have similar skulls to chimps, gorillas, and orangutans. They all have flat faces with well-developed jaws and large orbits to hold two forward-facing eyes.

BIG BRAINS

The scientific name for modern humans is *Homo sapiens*, which means "wise man." Humans have big brains, live in complex social groups, and make tools.

The braincase is large and rounded to make room for big brains.

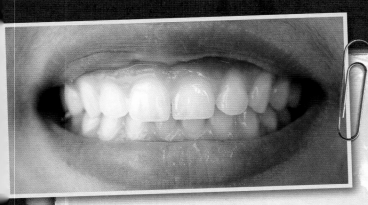

Teeth

An adult's mouth contains 32 teeth that allow humans to eat a wide range of food. Animals that eat many types of food, such as plants and meat, are called omnivores.

Human jaws are small but extremely powerful, and the muscles allow an incredible range of movement that enables speech.

CLEAR VISION

Human brains have large areas for language, thought, and learning new things. An area at the back of the brain is called the occipital lobe. This is where information from the eyes is turned into vision.

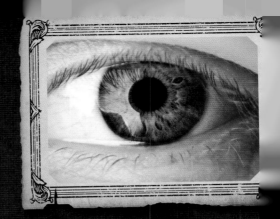

The eyes face forward, providing excellent sight. Humans can see in color and can judge distance, working out how far away objects a

Humans have flat faces with no snouts. The nose is constructed from cartilage, which cannot be seen in a bony skull.

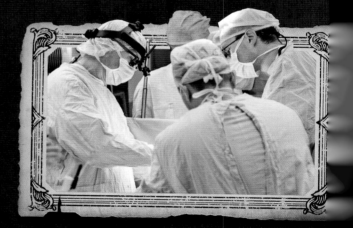

DELICATE OPERATIONS

Humans are able to carry out complicated actions, such as delicate surgery. This is because humans can learn, understand, and communicate with one another, as well as make and use tools.

BUILD YOUR OWN
HUMAN SKULL
AT THE END OF THE BOOK!

BRAIN AND NERVES

The outer layer, called the **cerebral cortex**, is folded to pack in extra neurons and connections.

BODIES are controlled by a system of billions of nerve cells, or neurons, most of which are packed together in brains and spinal cords.

NERVE CELLS

A neuron sends signals to other neurons along a long filament called an **axon**. It receives signals from other neurons along filaments called dendrites.

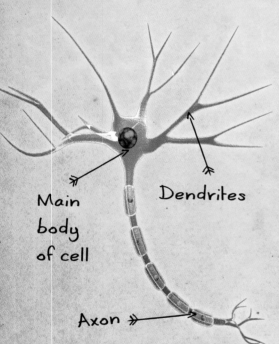

Main body of cell

Dendrites

Axon

The longest neurons in the body stretch from the base of the spine to the end of the big toes. In a tall person, the axons of these cells may be 3 feet long.

Prefrontal cortex

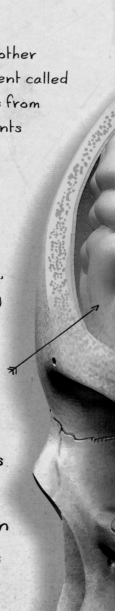

CONNECTED UP

Weighing just over 2 pounds, a brain contains about 100 billion neurons. Each neuron is connected to up to 10,000 other neurons. When a new fact or skill is learned, new connections form between neurons.

{ Brain hemispheres }

LEFT AND RIGHT
The brain is made of two hemispheres. The right hemisphere controls the movement of the left side of the body, while the left hemisphere controls the right side of the body.

CONTROL CENTER
As well as thinking, brains control movements and unconscious body processes such as breathing and digestion. The brain is connected to the rest of the body by nerve tissue called the spinal cord, which extends down the spine.

Nervous system

Visual cortex

Brain stem

Scanning the Brain
The bright areas of this MRI scan show which parts of the brain the person is using most. Different patterns appear depending on what the person is doing or thinking about.

Spinal cord

23

EYES

BRAINS create a visual picture of the world using information from the eyes. Vision is an important sense, and a large part of the brain is dedicated to producing it.

THREE DIMENSIONS

The image on the **retina** is in two dimensions, like a photograph. The brain turns this into a three-dimensional image. Having two eyes helps to do this. Each eye sends the brain an image from a slightly different angle. The brain combines these into one image with a sense of depth.

Eye muscle

Iris

Cornea

UPSIDE-DOWN IMAGE

Light enters the eyes through the **cornea**. Here, a lens focuses the light so that it forms a clear image on the retina at the back of the eye. The image on the retina is upside-down, but the brain corrects this so that the image is seen the right way up.

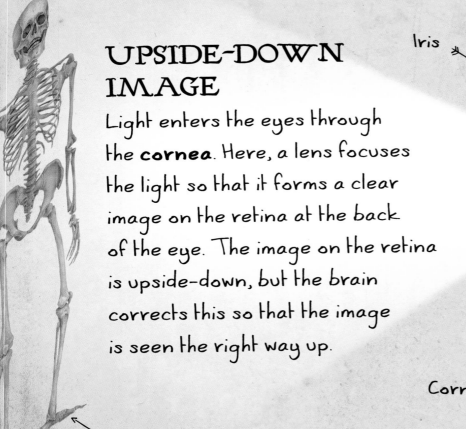

Object is visible because light rays are reflected off it.

BRIGHT OR DIM?

The hole that allows light through the cornea is called the pupil. Surrounding the pupil is the iris. The iris changes shape to make the pupil small in bright light to prevent being dazzled. In dim light, the pupil expands to allow more light in.

{ bright light }

{ dim light }

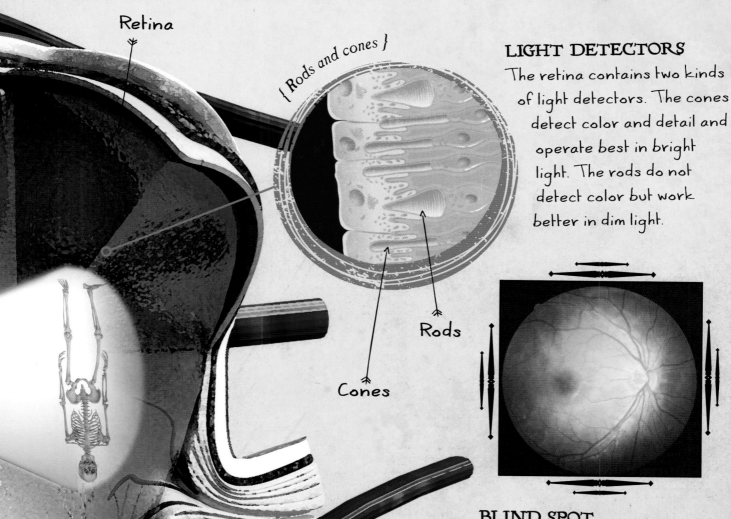

Retina

{ Rods and cones }

Rods

Cones

Optic nerve

LIGHT DETECTORS

The retina contains two kinds of light detectors. The cones detect color and detail and operate best in bright light. The rods do not detect color but work better in dim light.

BLIND SPOT

Messages are carried from the retina to the brain along the **optic nerve**. The area around the optic nerve cannot sense light, and this creates a blind spot. The brain "colors in" the blind spot so that it isn't noticeable.

EARS

EARS detect vibrations in the air. These vibrations are heard as sounds.

Ear flap

Ear canal carries sounds into the ear.

Sensitive Ears

Ears are sensitive to a huge range of loudness. The sound of a jet engine is 1,000 billion times louder than the quietest sound humans can hear. Very loud sounds can hurt ears as they make them vibrate too violently.

HEARING AIDS

Hearing aids work by making sounds much louder. A microphone picks up sounds and sends them to an amplifier. The amplifier makes the sounds much louder and sends them to the ear through a speaker.

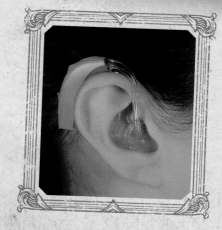

OUTER EAR

The outer ears are made from flexible **cartilage**. They collect sounds, which then make the eardrums vibrate.

MIDDLE EAR

In the middle ears, the three ossicle bones, called the hammer, the anvil, and the stirrup, carry vibrations from the eardrum to the inner ear. These are the smallest bones in the body. The stirrup is the smallest bone of all, just 0.1 inches across.

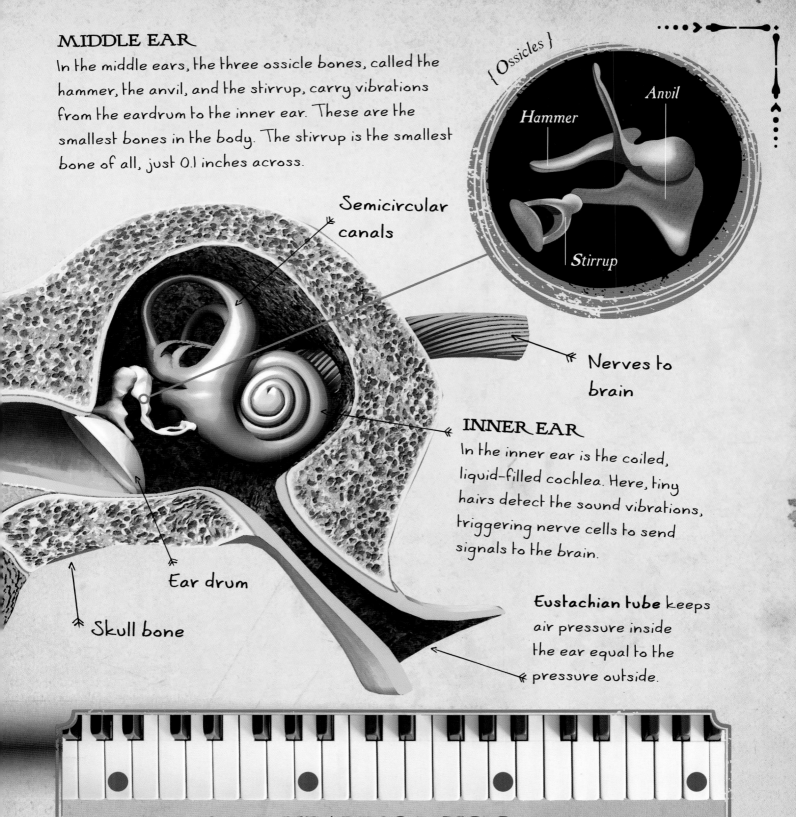

{ Ossicles }

Anvil

Hammer

Stirrup

Semicircular canals

Nerves to brain

Ear drum

Skull bone

INNER EAR

In the inner ear is the coiled, liquid-filled cochlea. Here, tiny hairs detect the sound vibrations, triggering nerve cells to send signals to the brain.

Eustachian tube keeps air pressure inside the ear equal to the pressure outside.

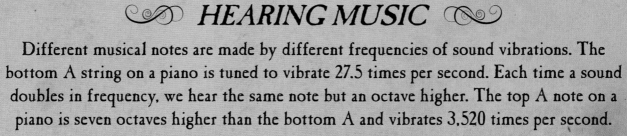

❧ HEARING MUSIC ❧

Different musical notes are made by different frequencies of sound vibrations. The bottom A string on a piano is tuned to vibrate 27.5 times per second. Each time a sound doubles in frequency, we hear the same note but an octave higher. The top A note on a piano is seven octaves higher than the bottom A and vibrates 3,520 times per second.

NOSE, TEETH, AND MOUTH

INSIDE the skull are large openings. Sensitive body parts in these openings help humans to smell, taste, and communicate with other people.

Skull bones

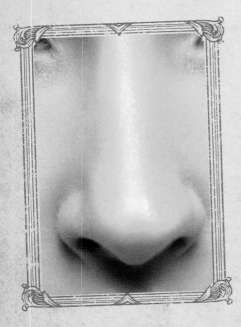

NOSE

Noses detect smells. Smells are molecules of substances in the air. The molecules are detected by receptors at the top of the nasal cavity. The **olfactory bulb** carries the smell signals to the brain.

Lips

Lips can be pulled into many different shapes to help humans eat and speak. The lips are packed with touch sensors, which send detailed information to the brain about everything that nears the mouth.

TEETH

Humans grow two sets of teeth during their lives. The first set, the milk teeth, fall out between the ages of six and 12, to be replaced by the larger permanent teeth. An adult has 32 teeth.

INCISORS

The eight incisors are used for biting.

MOLARS

The 12 molars and eight premolars are used for chewing and grinding food.

CANINES

The four canines are the sharpest teeth and are used for ripping and tearing.

Nasal cavity

Tongue

Teeth

Lower jawbone

{ Magnified taste buds }

TONGUE

The tongue is covered in about 10,000 taste buds, which taste five kinds of flavor: sweet, sour, salty, bitter, and umami (savory). All the complex flavors we can detect are different combinations of these five basic flavors. We also use our sense of smell to enhance the taste of food.

HORMONE SYSTEM

Hormones are chemical messengers released into the blood by organs called glands. They were first identified 100 years ago, and new ones are still being discovered.

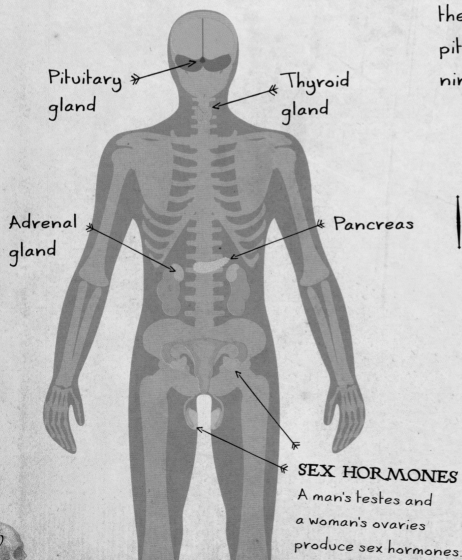

Pituitary gland

Thyroid gland

Adrenal gland

Pancreas

SEX HORMONES
A man's testes and a woman's ovaries produce sex hormones.

Pituitary gland

PITUITARY GLAND

Many of the body's glands are controlled by the pea-sized pituitary gland at the base of the brain. The pituitary gland releases nine different hormones.

INSULIN
The pancreas produces the hormone insulin, which tells the body to take in sugar from the blood. Diabetes results when the pancreas stops releasing insulin. Diabetics must monitor their blood sugar levels by taking blood tests.

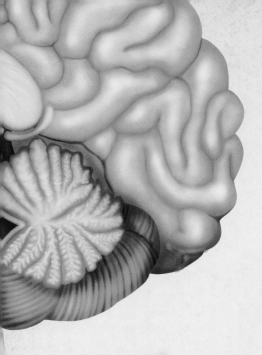

Growth Hormone

Pictured here with his father, American Robert Wadlow's pituitary gland released too much growth hormone. One of the tallest people to have ever lived, he was 8 feet 11.1 inches tall when he died at age 22.

FIGHT-OR-FLIGHT

When humans are in dangerous or exciting situations, the adrenal glands produce the hormone adrenaline. Heart rates increase, extra blood is directed to the muscles, and the pupils of the eyes enlarge.

THYROID GLAND

The butterfly-shaped thyroid gland in the neck releases two hormones that have a wide range of effects on the body, including regulating the burning of energy.

31

THE TORSO

THE torso contains many vital organs, including the heart, lungs, liver, stomach, and guts. Running the length of the torso is the backbone, to which the protective rib cage is attached.

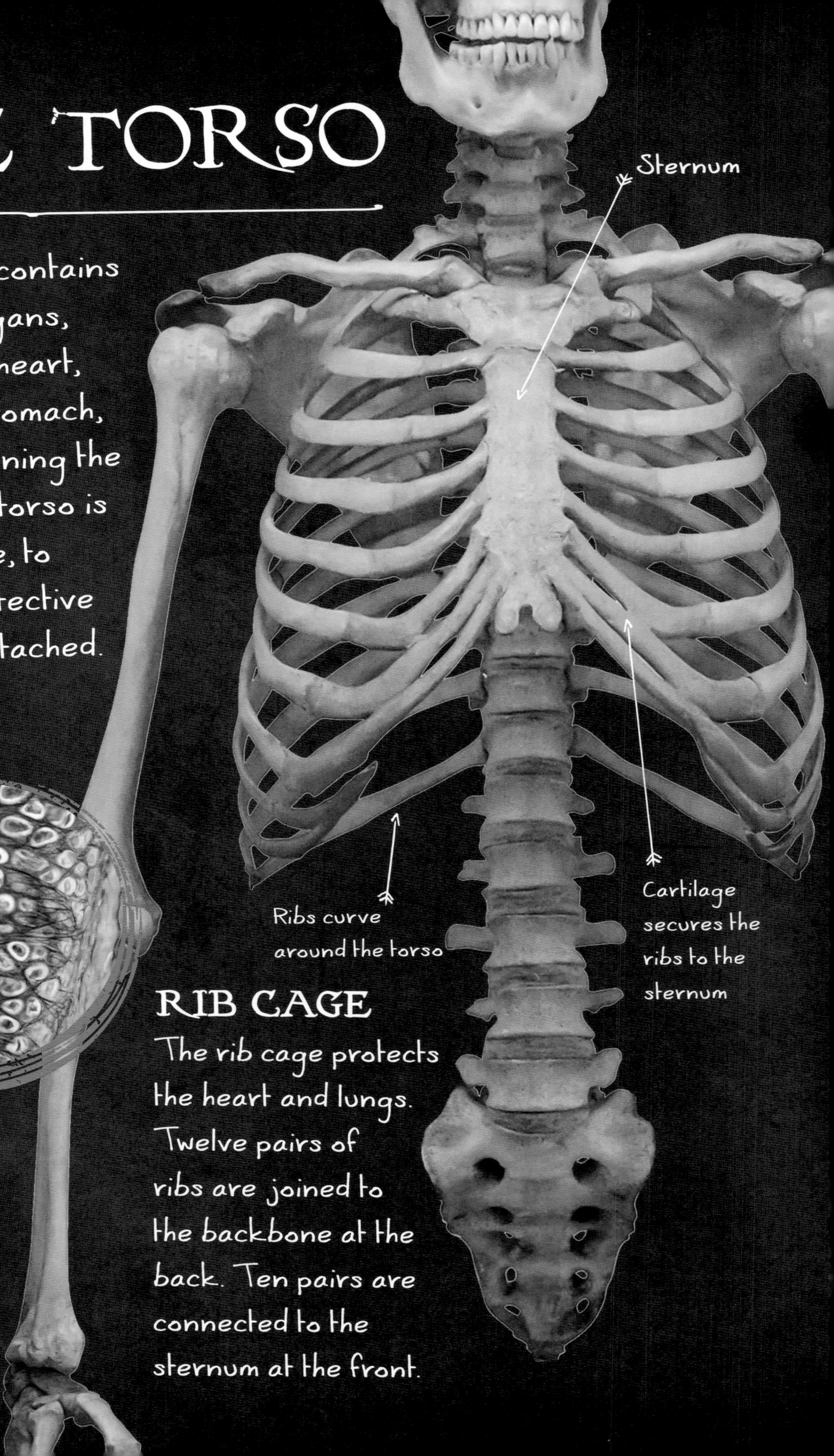

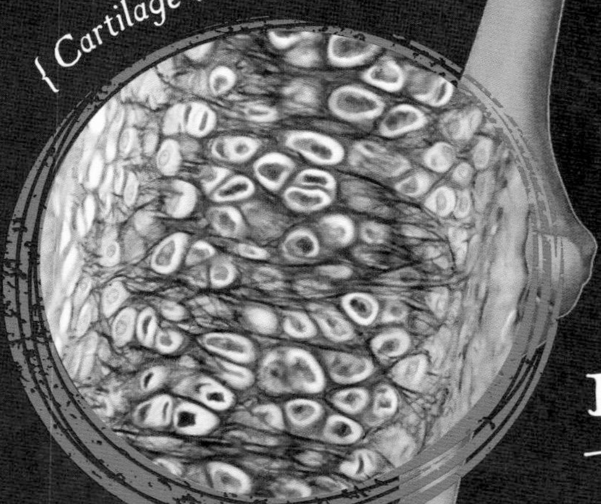

{ Cartilage tissue }

As well as linking the ribs and sternum, cartilage is found in the nose, ears, and in joints at the ends of some bones.

Sternum

Ribs curve around the torso

RIB CAGE

The rib cage protects the heart and lungs. Twelve pairs of ribs are joined to the backbone at the back. Ten pairs are connected to the sternum at the front.

Cartilage secures the ribs to the sternum

Seven cervical vertebrae support the neck and head.

Twelve thoracic vertebrae form joints with the twelve pairs of ribs.

BACKBONE

The backbone stretches from the head to the pelvis. It is made of 33 bones called vertebrae, which form a flexible S-shape. Running the length of the backbone is the spinal cord, which connects the brain to the rest of the body.

Flexibility

While the vertabrae can only move a little way in relation to each other, when they all act together, they can move a long way, making humans very flexible.

Five lumbar vertebrae are large and strong to bear the body's weight.

Five vertebrae of the sacrum are fused together to form a firm anchor for the hip bones.

Right at the end of the backbone is the coccyx, or tailbone, made of four fused vertebrae.

HEART AND BLOOD VESSELS

THE heart is a powerful muscle. It beats around 70 times per minute to pump blood around the body through blood vessels.

BLOOD PUMP

The heart has four chambers, two on the right and two on the left. The right side of the heart pumps blood to the lungs. The left side pumps blood to the rest of the body.

Right atrium

Right ventricle

Taking a Pulse

Each beat of the heart creates a pulse of blood through the arteries. The pulse can be felt by placing a finger on the wrist.

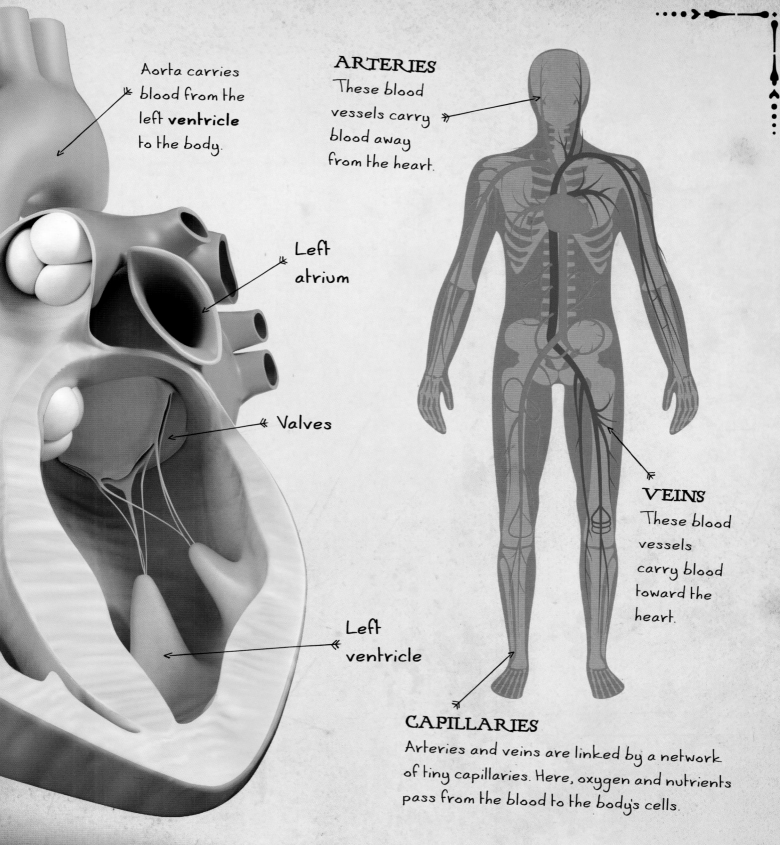

Aorta carries blood from the left **ventricle** to the body.

ARTERIES
These blood vessels carry blood away from the heart.

Left atrium

Valves

Left ventricle

VEINS
These blood vessels carry blood toward the heart.

CAPILLARIES
Arteries and veins are linked by a network of tiny capillaries. Here, oxygen and nutrients pass from the blood to the body's cells.

CONNECTING TO THE LUNGS
The pulmonary artery carries blood from the right ventricle to the lungs. Here the blood picks up oxygen and is returned to the left ventricle by the pulmonary veins. The oxygen-rich blood is then sent off through the body via the largest artery, the aorta.

BLOOD AND LYMPH

PUMPED around the body by the heart, blood carries oxygen and nutrients and also helps to protect against germs.

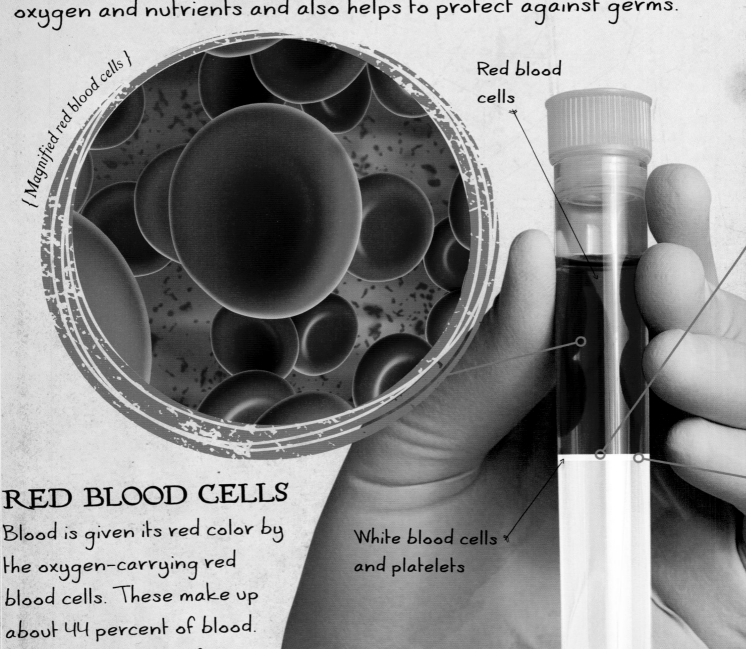

{ Magnified red blood cells }

Red blood cells

White blood cells and platelets

Plasma

RED BLOOD CELLS
Blood is given its red color by the oxygen-carrying red blood cells. These make up about 44 percent of blood. They carry oxygen from the lungs to the rest of the body.

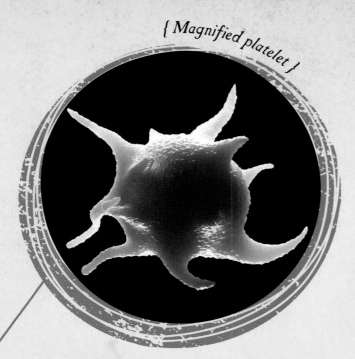

{ Magnified platelet }

PLATELETS

Platelets help heal wounds by creating blood clots.

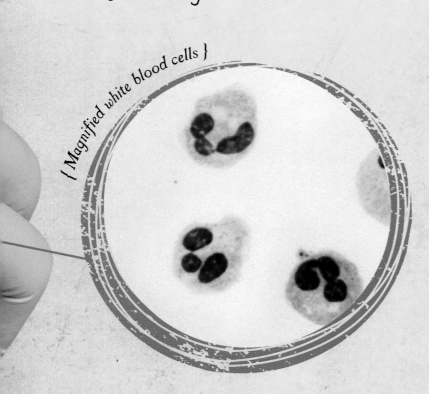

{ Magnified white blood cells }

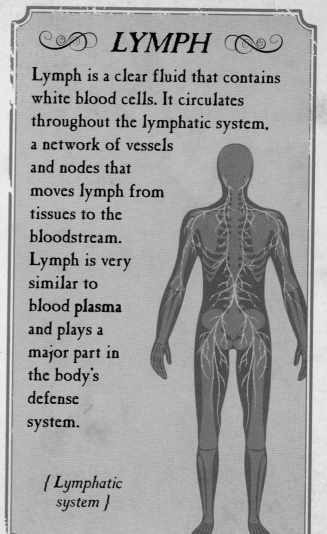

LYMPH

Lymph is a clear fluid that contains white blood cells. It circulates throughout the lymphatic system, a network of vessels and nodes that moves lymph from tissues to the bloodstream. Lymph is very similar to blood plasma and plays a major part in the body's defense system.

{ Lymphatic system }

WHITE BLOOD CELLS

The white blood cells form part of the body's defense system. They identify and destroy invading germs.

PLASMA

About 55 percent of blood is a liquid called plasma. It is about 90 percent water. Dissolved in the water are nutrients, waste matter, and hormones.

FIGHTING INFECTION

BODIES have a series of defenses against attack by germs. Together, these defenses form the body's immune system. The blood forms a vital part of this system.

EATING GERMS

Some white blood cells, called macrophages, hunt germs. When they find foreign objects, the macrophages engulf and destroy them. The cells also give out chemical signals to the rest of the body to warn of the presence of the germ.

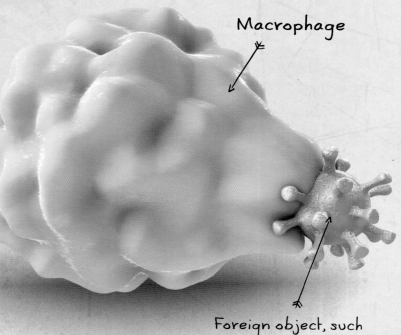

Macrophage

Foreign object, such as a bacterium or virus

VACCINES

Vaccines work by introducing a harmless form of a germ into the body. The immune system produces antibodies against the germ, meaning that it is ready to destroy the real thing if it appears. Vaccines have saved millions of lives and virtually wiped out diseases such as polio, tuberculosis, and smallpox.

HEALING A WOUND ⚜

The skin protects us from germs. When we cut our skin, our blood gets to work creating a protective scab to stop infection.

{ Platelets }   { Fibrin }   { Bacteria }   { Scab }   { Scab }

{ Wound }

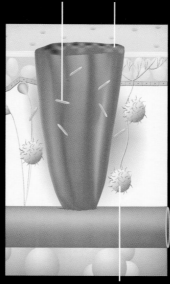

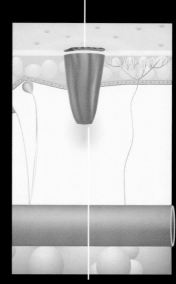

{ Blood vessels }   { White blood cells }   { Freshly healed tissue}

1. Platelets in the blood stick together to stop the bleeding. Protein fibers called fibrin form a mesh around the wound, which captures red blood cells to form a clot.

2. A scab forms on the surface of the clot. This protects the wound while tissues heal underneath. White blood cells move in to remove bacteria.

3. The wound gets smaller as new tissues are repaired and built.

Macrophages completely engulf bacteria and foreign objects.

ATTACKING FORCE

Macrophages can attack bacteria, viruses, fungi, and small parasites —anything that should not be there.

THE LUNGS

THE lungs are two large organs that take in oxygen from the air and expel carbon dioxide. Air is breathed through the nose and mouth.

ESSENTIAL TO LIFE

The body needs a constant supply of oxygen to create a chemical reaction that releases the energy stored in the sugars and fats in cells. This reaction is called respiration and produces carbon dioxide, which is expelled from our bodies when it is breathed out.

The right lung is slightly larger than the left.

BREATHING

When breathing in, a muscle called the diaphragm contracts and pushes down, and muscles between the ribs contract and pull the rib cage out. This expands the chest, pushing air through the trachea and into the lungs.

{ Breathing in }

When breathing out, the diaphragm and rib muscles relax. The lungs shrink and air is pushed out of the nose and mouth.

{ Breathing out }

Larynx

MAKING SOUNDS

On its way from the mouth to the lungs, air passes through the larynx, where speech sounds are made. As air is breathed out, the vocal cords in the larynx vibrate, producing sound. Muscles pull on the vocal cords, changing them so that they make different sounds.

Trachea

BRONCHIAL TREE

Inside the lungs, the airways subdivide into smaller and smaller branches called bronchi. This creates a large surface area in contact with blood vessels. The total surface area of the lungs is up to 810 square feet, about half the size of a tennis court.

Bronchus

{ Alveoli }

ALVEOLI

At the ends of the bronchi, oxygen passes into the bloodstream through the walls of tiny air bags called alveoli. At the same time, carbon dioxide from the blood passes into the air in the alveoli to be breathed out.

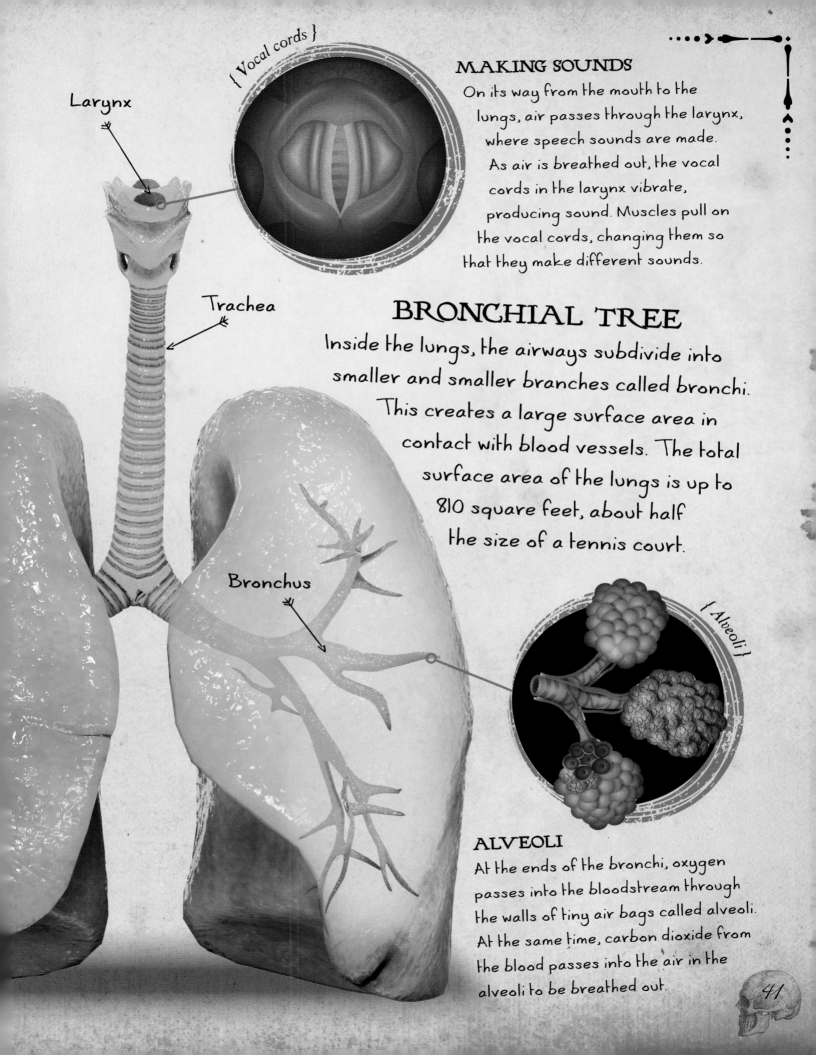

PELVIS

THE pelvis joins the legs to the backbone. It also provides support to the organs found in the abdomen—the area between the chest and the legs.

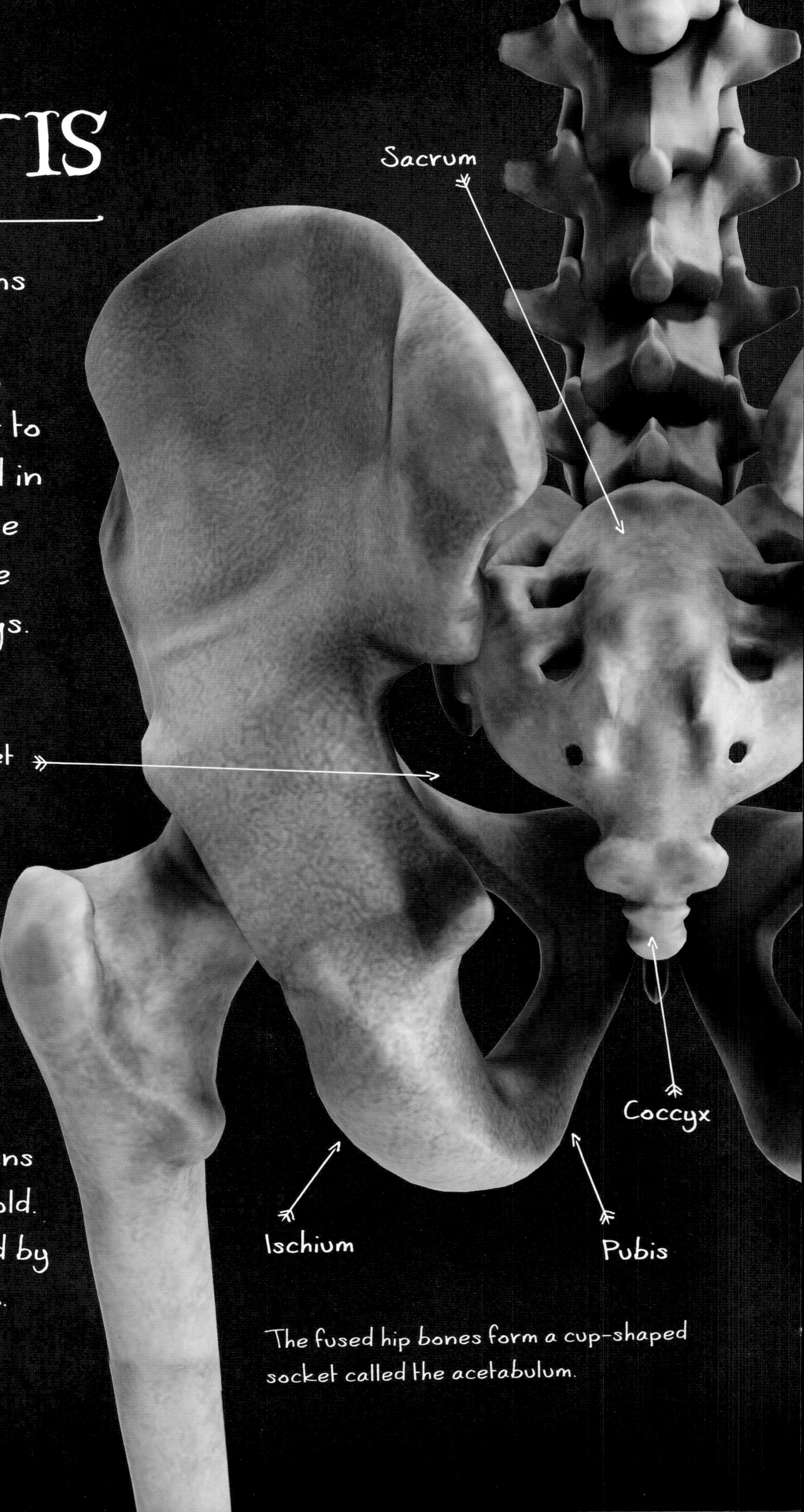

FUSING BONES

The hip bones are formed of three bones that start to fuse together when humans are about 15 years old. They are fully fused by the time they are 25.

Sacrum

Pelvic inlet

Coccyx

Ischium

Pubis

The fused hip bones form a cup-shaped socket called the acetabulum.

The hip bones are joined to the backbone by the sacrum.

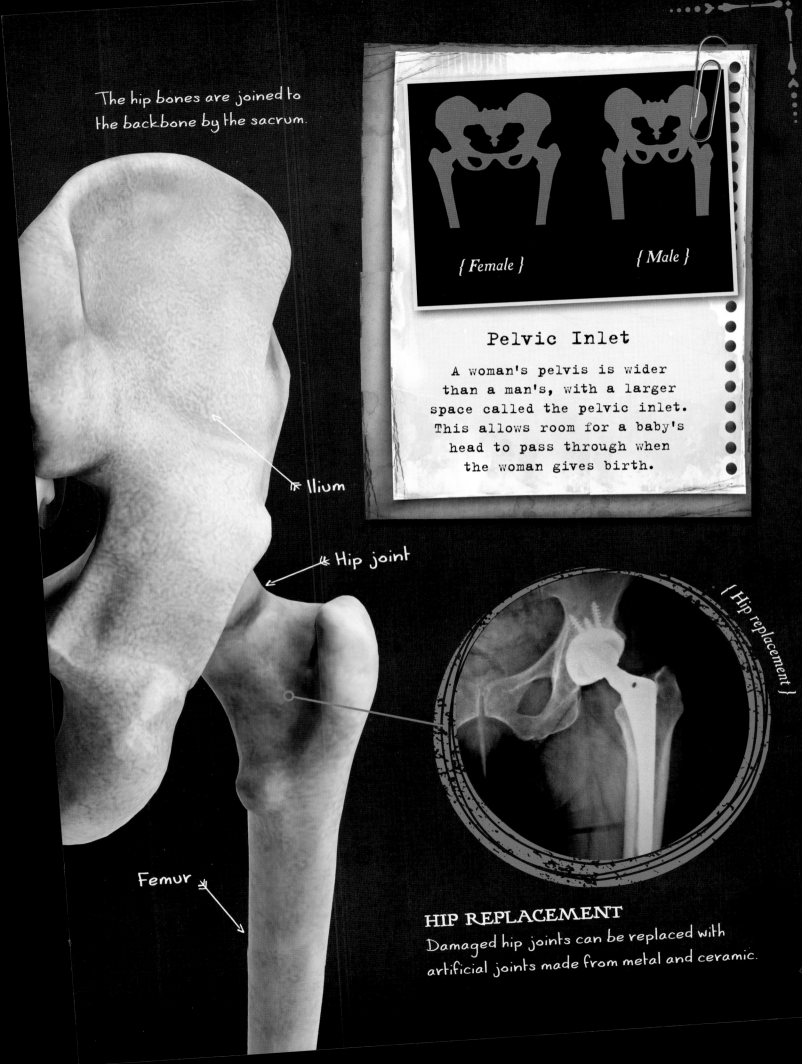

{ Female }   { Male }

Pelvic Inlet

A woman's pelvis is wider than a man's, with a larger space called the pelvic inlet. This allows room for a baby's head to pass through when the woman gives birth.

Ilium

Hip joint

{ Hip replacement }

Femur

HIP REPLACEMENT
Damaged hip joints can be replaced with artificial joints made from metal and ceramic.

THE DIGESTIVE SYSTEM

BEFORE a body can use the food that is eaten, it needs to break it down into simpler substances. The substances are then absorbed into the blood. This process is called **digestion**.

Tongue

MOUTH
Digestion begins in the mouth, where food is mixed with saliva and chewed before it is swallowed.

Oesophagus

STOMACH
Food spends about three hours in the stomach, where it is churned into a thick liquid called chyme.

LIVER
The liver stores nutrients and destroys poisons. Nutrient-rich blood from the small intestine passes through the liver, which sends nutrients that are needed to the rest of the body, and stores others.

{ Liver tissue }

The small intestine measures 20 feet from end to end.

SMALL INTESTINE

The chyme passes into the twisted small intestine, where the food is fully digested over about six hours.

{ Bacteria }

GUT FLORA

Inside the intestines are trillions of bacteria, known as gut flora, that help to digest the food.

Anus

LARGE INTESTINE

The undigested waste passes into the large intestine, where it is stored for up to 40 hours before it is expelled through the anus as feces.

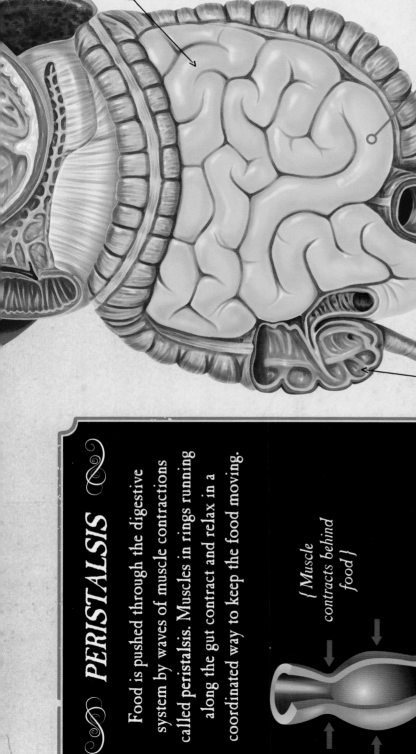

✺ PERISTALSIS ✺

Food is pushed through the digestive system by waves of muscle contractions called peristalsis. Muscles in rings running along the gut contract and relax in a coordinated way to keep the food moving.

{ Muscle contracts behind food }

{ Muscle relaxes around food }

FILTERING THE BLOOD

THE urinary system filters the blood, removing waste and excess water and salt. The kidneys turn these unwanted substances into urine, which is expelled from the body as pee.

Kidney >>

Ureter >>

Pelvis >>

Bladder >>

BLADDER

Urine passes from the kidneys into the bladder. Here, it is stored until it is removed from the body through the urethra.

Urethra >>

Adrenal
gland

Renal
artery

KIDNEYS

Blood passes from the renal artery into the kidneys, which filter out unwanted substances to create urine. The kidneys are constantly at work, making a trickle of urine.

{ Kidney structure }

TINY STRUCTURES

Each kidney contains millions of tiny structures called nephrons, where the blood is filtered, keeping what is needed and removing waste substances.

Filtered blood passes back into capillaries.

∾ URINE ∾

Urine is about 95 percent water. About 2 percent is a waste substance called urea. The rest is made up of smaller amounts of a range of waste chemicals.

The waste chemicals found in urine include ammonia, sulphate, phosphate, chloride, magnesium, calcium, potassium, sodium, creatinine, and uric acid.

WATER LEVEL

The amount of water released in urine is controlled by the pituitary gland under the brain. The gland releases the hormone ADH when we are dehydrated. This tells the kidneys to reabsorb more water.

REPRODUCTIVE SYSTEM

REPRODUCTION is the creation of new life. The reproductive system is the only body system that is different for males and females. Men produce sperm and women produce eggs. A sperm **fertilizes** an egg, which grows into a baby in the uterus.

MALE SYSTEM

The male sex organs are made up of the penis and the two testes. Millions of sperm are made inside the testes, and released through the penis.

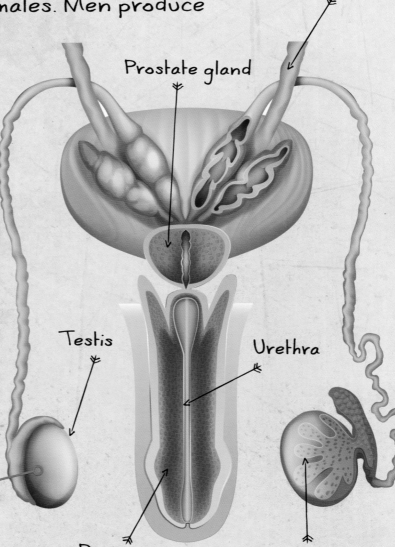

Ureter

Prostate gland

Testis

Urethra

Penis

Testis tubes produce sperm

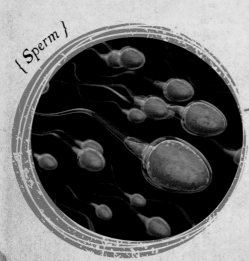

{ Sperm }

The tiny sperm are about 0.002 inches in length, with long, whiplike tails.

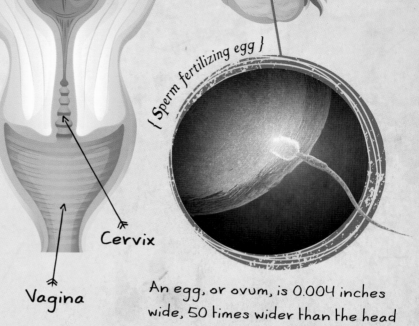

Uterus

Fallopian tube

Ovary

FEMALE SYSTEM

The female sex organs are made up of two ovaries and fallopian tubes, the uterus, or womb, and the vagina. Once a month, the ovaries release an egg. If the egg is fertilized by a sperm, it travels to the uterus, where it grows into a baby.

{ Sperm fertilizing egg }

Cervix

Vagina

An egg, or ovum, is 0.004 inches wide, 50 times wider than the head of a sperm.

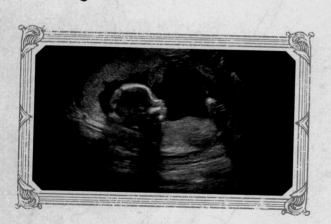

IN THE WOMB

The fertilized egg, called a zygote, starts to divide as it travels toward the womb. It attaches itself to the soft lining of the womb, where it develops into a fetus. The baby is born about 38 weeks later. Ultrasound scans produce an image of a fetus in the womb.

FEEDING

A new-born baby is entirely dependent on its parents. For the first few months of its life, the baby feeds on its mother's milk, which is produced by special organs called mammary glands in the mother's breasts.

ARMS AND SHOULDERS

THE arms and shoulders contain a range of flexible joints and muscles that provide power and control to the hands and fingers. Three very mobile joints—the shoulders, elbows, and wrists—provide a huge range of movement.

Clavicle

Humerus

Scapula

SHOULDERS

The shoulder is made of three bones: the clavicle, or collarbone, the scapula, or shoulder blade, and the humerus. Together they allow for a wide range of movement. The flat, triangular scapula resembles the blade of a trowel. It can slide around the torso, helping to give the arm the biggest possible range of movement.

Supination

Pronation

ROTATING WRISTS

The forearm contains two bones, the radius and ulna. These bones cross over one another when we rotate our wrists. The wrist is rotated by a pair of muscles called the supinator and pronator muscles.

Wrist

Radius

Elbow

The forearm contains 20 different muscles. Fifteen of these muscles are to move the hand and wrist, while five move the forearm itself.

Ulna

Shoulder Joint

The humerus is connected to the scapula at a flexible ball-and-socket joint, which allows humans to swing the arms freely. The joint can become dislocated when the ball comes out of the socket. This is very painful, but the humerus can be snapped back into place.

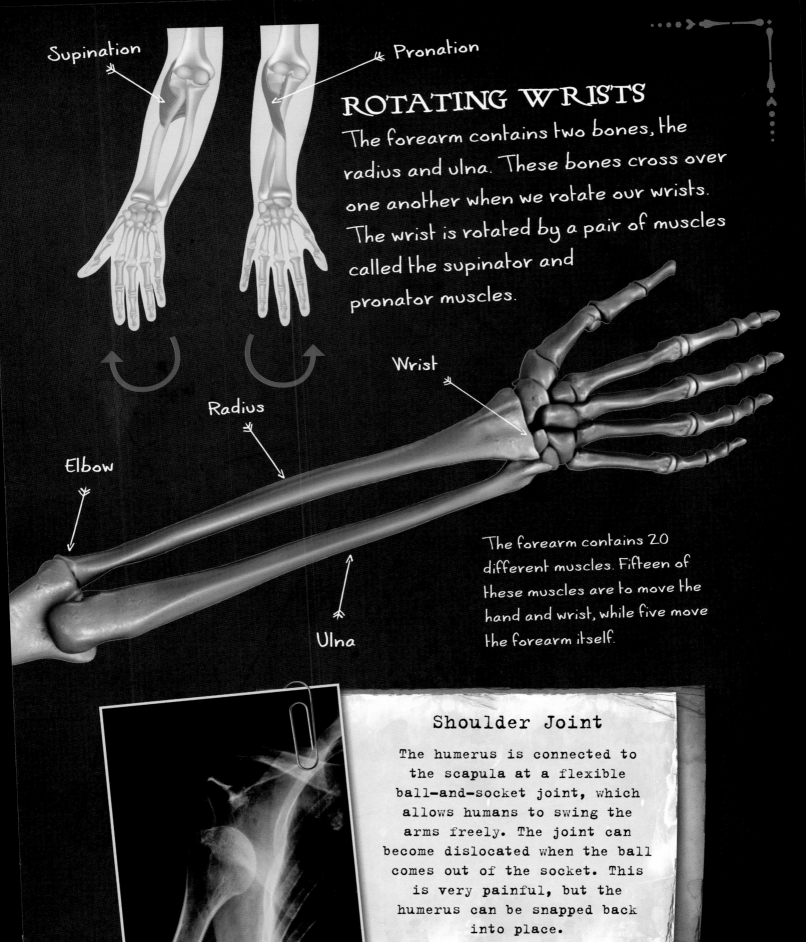

MUSCLES

WITHOUT muscles, the human body would not be able to move. Muscles are made of cells that can contract (become shorter) and exert a pulling force.

CARDIAC MUSCLE

The wall of the heart is made of cardiac muscle, which keeps the heart beating.

Pectoral muscle

Biceps

Quadriceps

SKELETAL MUSCLES

These are the muscles that move bones. Muscles can only pull in one direction. For this reason, skeletal muscles always work in pairs. The biceps and triceps work together to bend and straighten the arm at the elbow.

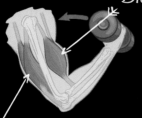

Biceps contracts

Triceps relaxes

Triceps contracts

Biceps relaxes

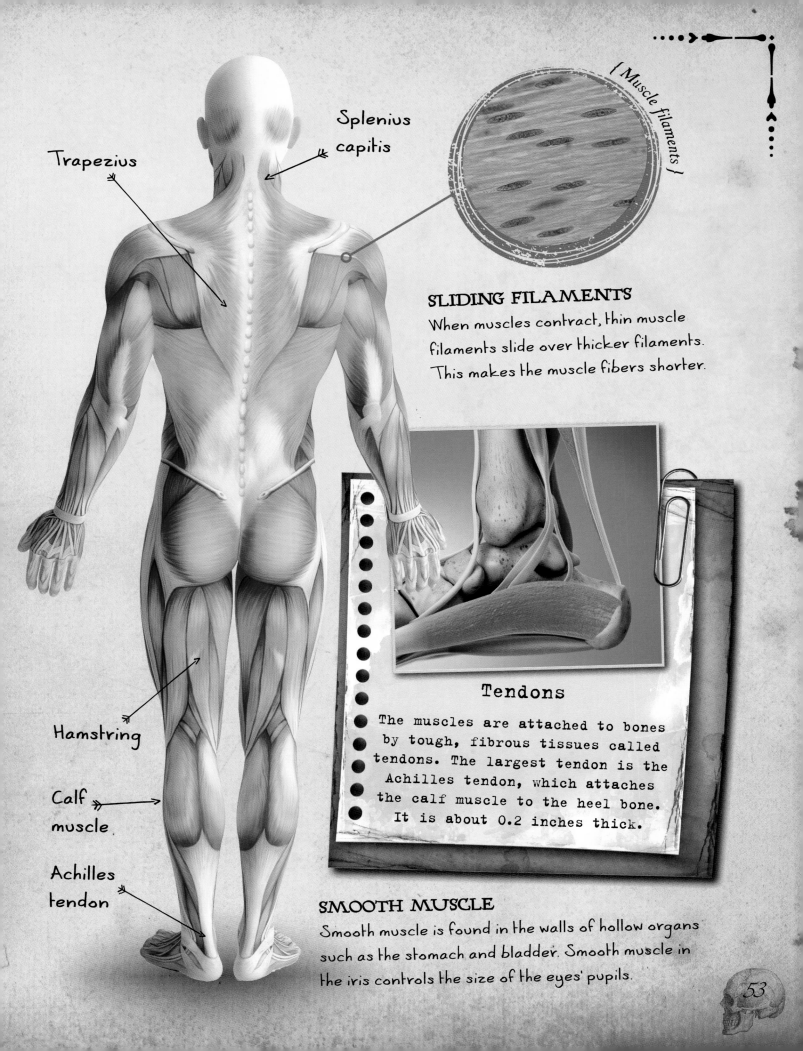

Trapezius

Splenius
capitis

{ Muscle filaments }

SLIDING FILAMENTS
When muscles contract, thin muscle
filaments slide over thicker filaments.
This makes the muscle fibers shorter.

Tendons

The muscles are attached to bones
by tough, fibrous tissues called
tendons. The largest tendon is the
Achilles tendon, which attaches
the calf muscle to the heel bone.
It is about 0.2 inches thick.

Hamstring

Calf
muscle

Achilles
tendon

SMOOTH MUSCLE
Smooth muscle is found in the walls of hollow organs
such as the stomach and bladder. Smooth muscle in
the iris controls the size of the eyes' pupils.

53

HANDS

THE human hand contains 27 bones. A system of muscles gives fine control and allows humans to pick up and manipulate objects.

The eight short carpal bones in the wrist connect the hand to the arm.

The muscles that bend and straighten the fingers and thumb are located in the forearm. Flexor muscles bend the fingers, while extensor muscles straighten them.

Carpal bones

MUSCLE CONTROL

The hands are controlled by a complicated set of muscles, some of which are in the hand and others in the forearm.

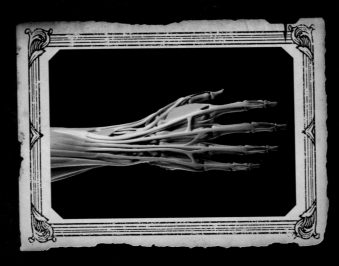

Metacarpal bones

The five metacarpal bones connect the wrist to the fingers and thumb.

OPPOSABLE THUMB

The joint at the base of the thumb is much more flexible than the joints of the fingers, allowing it to manipulate objects delicately.

↖ Thumb

Sensitive Fingers

Fingers are packed with touch sensors. We can feel a bump just 0.008 inches high by touching it. Fingers become even more sensitive when they are dragged across a surface, and can sense wrinkles in the surface that are a few millionths of an inch across.

Each finger is made of three phalange bones. The thumb is made of two phalange bones.

↑ Phalanges

The muscles in the hand give the thumb its flexible movement so that the palms can open and close.

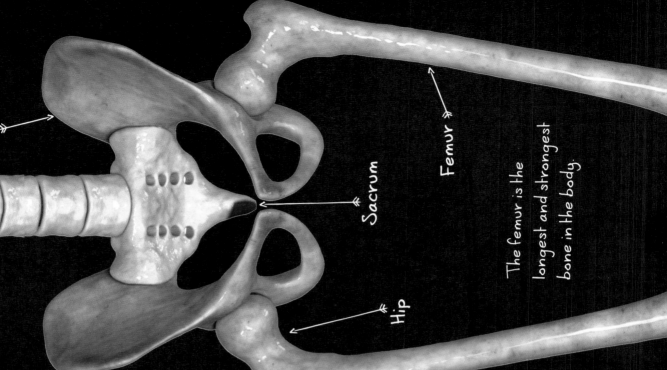

Pelvis

Sacrum

Hip

Femur

The femur is the longest and strongest bone in the body.

HIPS AND LEGS

STRETCHING down from the pelvis are the lower limbs, or legs. They contain the strongest and most powerful bones and muscles in the body. These allow the body to stand upright while the joints at the hips, knees, and ankles allow humans to bend, squat, walk, and run.

GLUTES

The gluteus maximus, or buttock muscles, are the largest muscles in the body. They help to move the hips and thighs and keep the body upright as it moves about.

Fibula

Patella
(kneecap)

Tibia

Knee
cartilage

The patella sits
over the kneecap
and protects this
complicated joint
from knocks
and bumps.

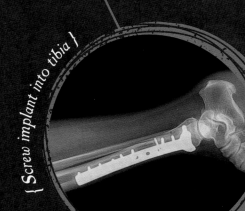

{ Screw implant into tibia }

Knee Joint

The knee joint is the most
complex joint in the body. It
is a modified hinge joint that
allows the leg to bend and
straighten, but also to
rotate a little.

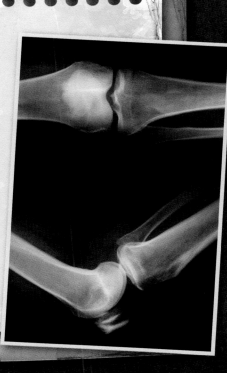

HEALING
FRACTURE

This X-ray shows a fractured
tibia that has been pinned
together. The pins ensure that
the bone stays fixed in the right
shape as it heals.

WALKING AND RUNNING

HUMANS are one of only a few mammals that can stand and move on two legs for long periods of time. While a slow walk may only use muscles in the hips and legs, sprinting uses muscles throughout the body so that movement is as easy as possible.

Muscles in the torso work to twist the body.

Muscles in the upper leg work to bend and straighten the limb during a run.

HIGH HURDLES

In training, hurdlers work to make their hip joints as flexible as possible. This allows them to bring their legs up over the hurdles while running.

The back leg pushes off from the ball of the foot to take the next step.

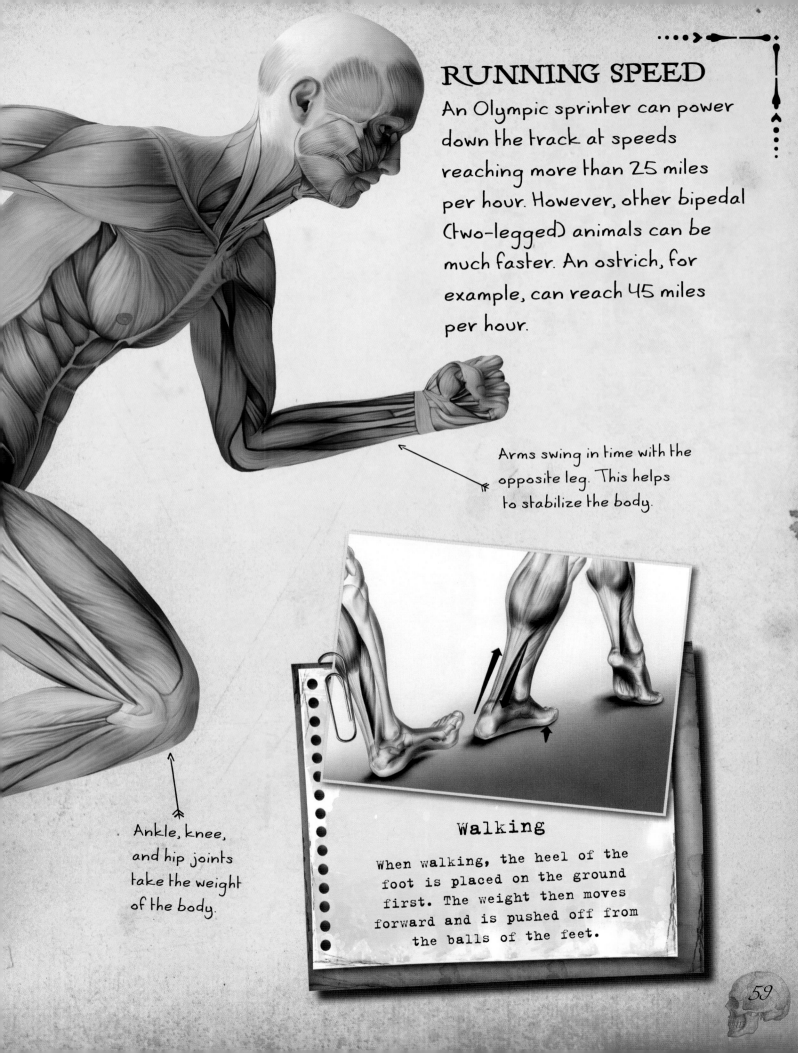

RUNNING SPEED

An Olympic sprinter can power down the track at speeds reaching more than 25 miles per hour. However, other bipedal (two-legged) animals can be much faster. An ostrich, for example, can reach 45 miles per hour.

Arms swing in time with the opposite leg. This helps to stabilize the body.

Ankle, knee, and hip joints take the weight of the body.

Walking

When walking, the heel of the foot is placed on the ground first. The weight then moves forward and is pushed off from the balls of the feet.

FEET

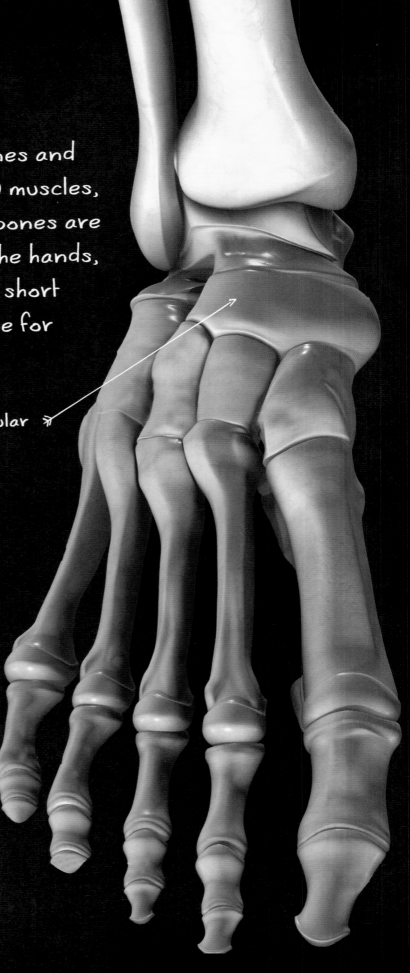

EACH foot contains 26 bones and is controlled by more than 100 muscles, tendons, and ligaments. The bones are arranged in a similar way to the hands, but they are less flexible, with short toes. This provides a firm base for standing and running.

Navicular ➹

ON TIP TOES

The tough ligaments that hold the foot bones together and the powerful muscles at the back of the lower leg allow humans to lift their whole body weight onto the toes. Ballet dancers have special shoes that allow them to dance on the very tips of their toes.

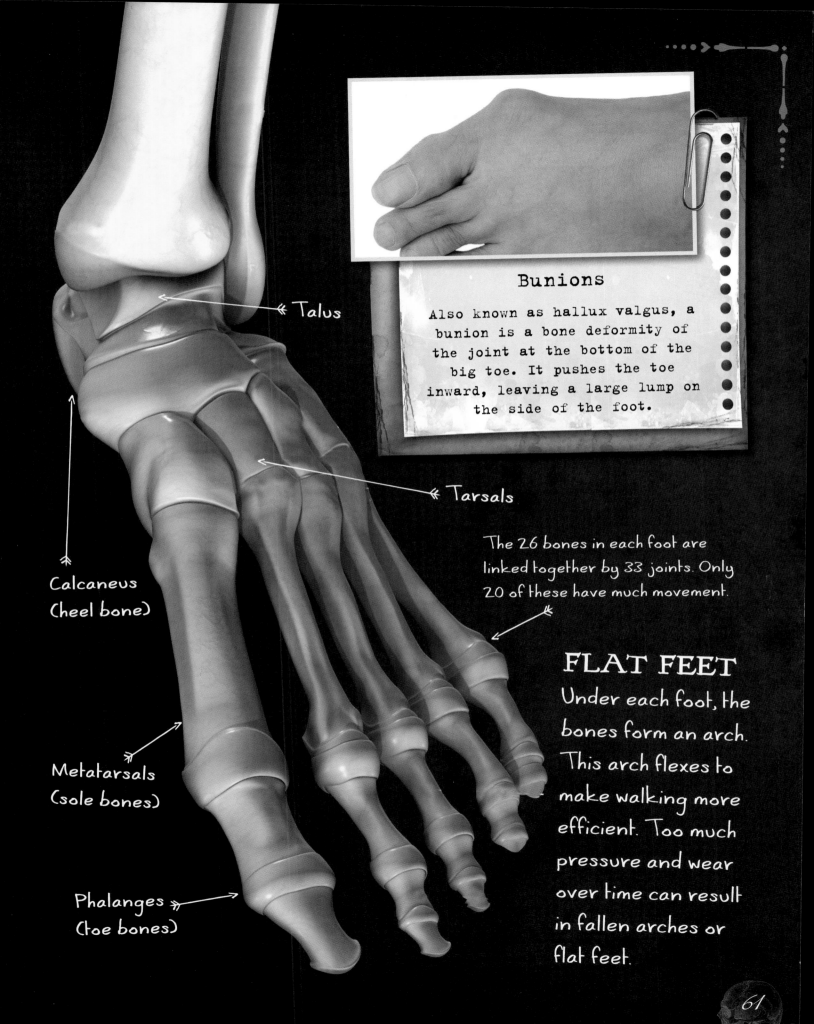

Talus

Tarsals

The 26 bones in each foot are linked together by 33 joints. Only 20 of these have much movement.

Calcaneus
(heel bone)

Metatarsals
(sole bones)

Phalanges
(toe bones)

FLAT FEET

Under each foot, the bones form an arch. This arch flexes to make walking more efficient. Too much pressure and wear over time can result in fallen arches or flat feet.

GLOSSARY

AXON
Long extension on a nerve cell that carries nerve signals from the cell body.

CARTILAGE
Strong, flexible substance found at the ends of some bones and in the ears and nose.

CELL
Smallest part of a living thing that can function independently.

CEREBRAL CORTEX
Wrinkled outer layer of the brain.

CHROMOSOMES
Part of a cell that contains the genetic information that tells the cell how to function.

COMPACT BONE
Type of dense bone tissue that's usually found near the outside of bones.

CORNEA
Transparent layer that covers the outside of each eye.

DERMIS
Found beneath the epidermis, this is the layer of the skin containing blood vessels, hair follicles, and nerve endings.

DIGESTION
Breaking food down into its simplest parts so that these can be absorbed by the body and used to produce energy, repair cells, and for growth.

EPIDERMIS
Outer layer of the skin.

EUSTACHIAN TUBE
Thin tube linking the middle ear with the back of the mouth and nose.

FERTILIZE
When a sperm and an egg fuse and a young living organism begins to develop.

FRACTURE
Crack or break in a bone.

HORMONE
Chemical produced by glands around the body which tells certain body parts how to behave.

IRIS
Colored ring at the front of the eye. It changes size to make the pupil bigger or smaller.

JOINT
Part where two bones meet.

LIGAMENTS
Tough strips of fibers that hold bones together in joints.

MARROW
Fatty substance found inside some bones.

MEMBRANE
Outer covering of something. A cell membrane regulates substances moving in and out of the cell.

MITOCHONDRIA
Tiny structures inside a cell where energy is produced.

NUCLEUS
Structure inside a cell that contains the genetic information.

OLFACTORY BULB
Structure in the roof of the nose where smells are turned into nerve signals and sent to the brain.

OPTIC NERVE
Nerve that carries signals from the eye.

ORGAN
Part of the body that carries out a specific role.

PERISTALSIS
Wavelike contraction of muscles along the intestines, which pushes food through the gut.

PLASMA
Straw-colored liquid that contains blood cells.

PUPIL
Hole at the front of each eyeball, through which light enters.

REPRODUCTION
Production of a new living organism.

RETINA
Layer at the back of the eyeball.

SPONGY BONE
Type of bone tissue that contains lots of holes, giving it a spongy appearance.

SYSTEM
Collection of organs and other body parts that carries out a job within the body.

TENDONS
Tough fibers that connect muscles to bones.

TISSUE
Collection of similar cells that have the same function.

VACCINE
Substance that contains a harmless form of a disease. It is given to a person to stop them catching that disease.

VENTRICLE
Lower chamber in the heart from which blood is pumped out into the arteries.

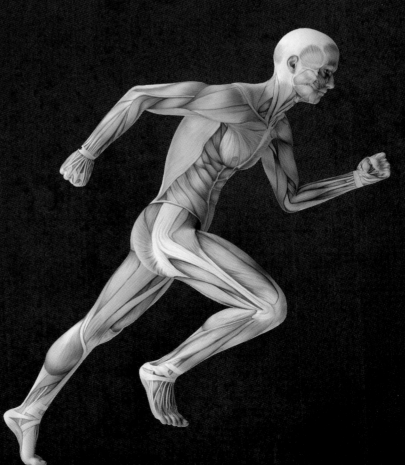

INDEX

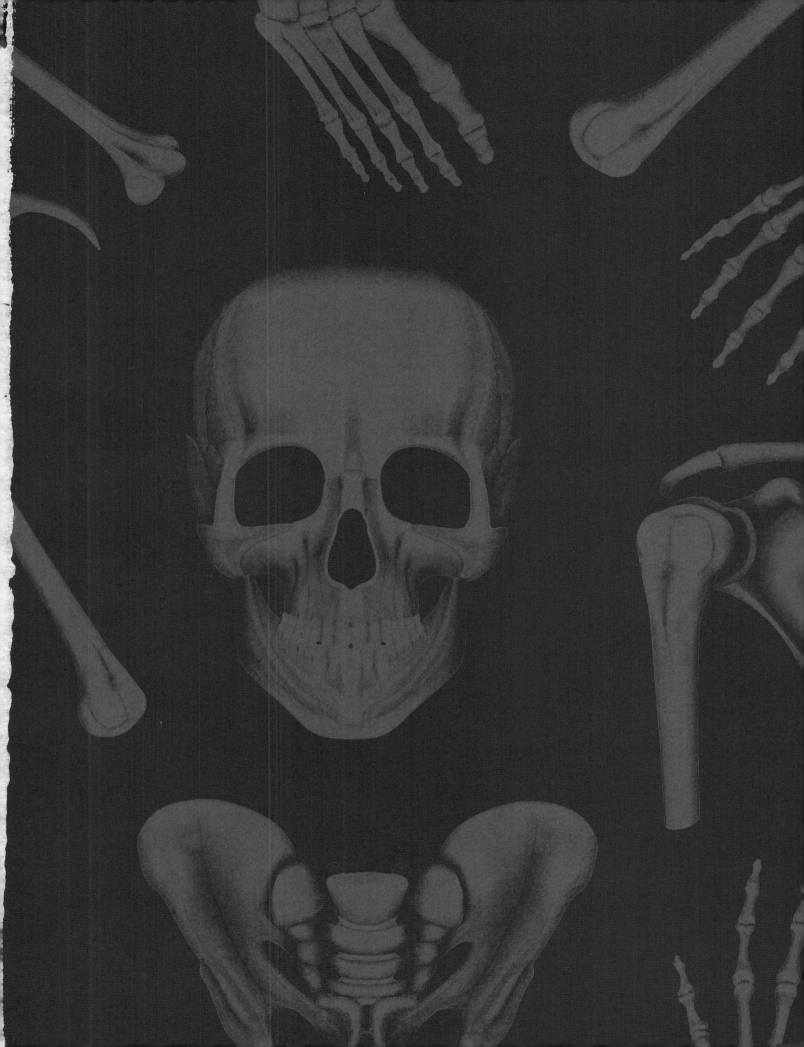

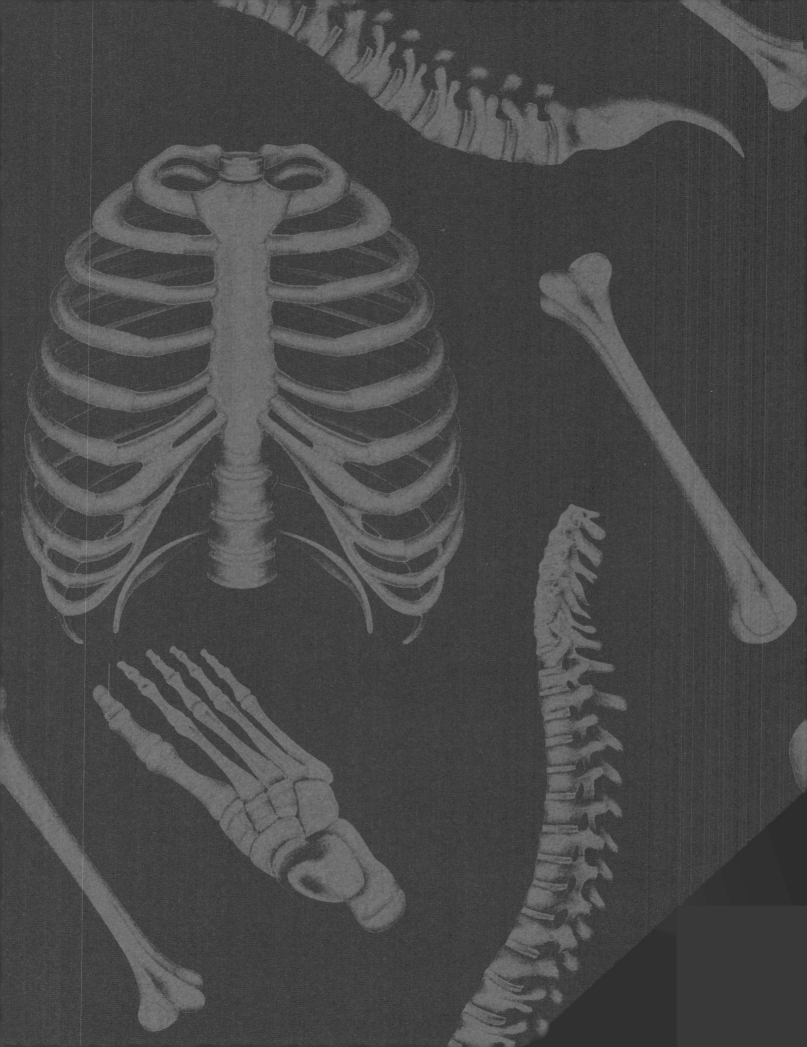